I0190984

SSHHH…It's A Secret!

How to write your

AMAZING

book fast!

Dr. Leah McCray

Sshhh…It's A Secret!
How to write your amazing book fast!

Dr. Leah McCray

Copyright © 2016 by Leah McCray. All Rights Reserved.

Published by:
Anointed Words Publishing Company

All Rights Reserved. No part of this book may be used or reproduced in any manner whatsoever without the expressed written permission of the author. Address all inquiries to:

Email: mail@awpubco.com www.awpubco.com

ISBN: 978-0-9977397-1-8
Printed in the United States of America

Contents

Setting goals is fun and games. Going after them is another matter. Without perspiration to match your inspiration, your dream imagined will turn into a dream deferred. Where do you stand on the road to execution of your God-given idea?

- Mark Batterson.

How to Use This Book

Very simple. Gather a pad, pencil, your imagination and your ideas for your book. You will find that there is space provided within these pages to write down your initial thoughts and ideas, as they come to you, but if you're like me, a few spaced lines will not be nearly enough; hence, your paper pad or Ipad ☺.

As you go through this workbook, you will find many tools and tricks of the writing trade to will help you organize your thoughts and put your words into proper form and presentation. You will find that once you have a formula for writing, your writing will come much easier and be much more enjoyable. From one formally frustrated writer to another, there is nothing like having a writing roadmap.

So, stop stressing and get back to finishing (or starting) that wonderful book that is bursting to come out of you. Make today the day you purpose to get it done fast. This little book will help you achieve that goal in no time.

First Things First

First question; what type of book are you planning to write?

1. A writing that you have created about people or things that have not happened, whether a short story or longer, it is FICTION.

2. A writing based on real events and/or real people, it is NON-FICTION.

3. A writing to help the reader solve a particular problem or issue would be a SELF-HELP / SELF-DEVELOPMENT / SELF-IMPROVEMENT book.

4. Books geared toward the entertaining or the creative instructing of children are CHILDREN'S BOOKS.

5. A self-written account of a person's life is an AUTOBIOGRAPHY.

6. An account of a person's life written by someone else is a BIOGRAPHY.

7. A writing meant to be a factual account or reporting is a DOCUMENTARY.

So, first things first…write down the type of book you plan to write:

_____

Now answer the following:

1) What is it that you want to accomplish by writing your book?

_____

_____

_____

_____

2) What is the one or two problems that you want to solve? (Remember the bigger or more widespread the problem, the more people in your pool of potential buyers. However, don't discount a smaller targeted area of need).

_____

_____

_____

3) Is there a need to solve this problem? Why? Why not?

_____

_____

_____

4) If you wrestled with answering #3 try this! On the blanks below write a list of names of people that you believe would want to read your book?

1.   6.

2.   7.

3.   8.

4.   9.

5.   10.

If you are wrestling with question #1, see if any of these categories jump out at you:

Self-Help / Self-Development / Self-Improvement:
Loving God

Growing in Areas of Spirituality

Being a great leader

Getting and Staying
Healthy
Healthy Weight Loss
Dealing with Loss
Fighting Addiction
Realizing Your Dreams
Setting & Achieving Goals
Walking in Boldness

Children's Book:
Learning Colors
Numbers
Making Friends
Following Directions
Building the child's imagination

**Autobiography /
Biography:**
Showing others how to overcome
Conquering Fear & Failure
How you made it in business
Keys to your success
Learning to lead
Mistakes that you've made
Keeping your integrity in…..

Documentary:
Teach or inform about a person, place or event in history

4 Simple Questions

Answer these 4 simple questions:

1. *Why You?*
2. *Why This?*
3. *Why Now?*
4. *Why Me?*

The answers to these questions will reveal your purpose and passion in writing this book and help you transmit that passion to your readers.

Why You?

Why should the reader pick up this book and spend time reading it. How will this book help them solve some problem? Show them a problem that they may not even realize they need relief from. What is the reason that they need to read your book? It's all about them, not you. Let your language reflect that... use "you" not "I's here.

Why This?

Why is this *book* the one that they should read instead of all the others that are written on this subject? Why is this the one that can answer their questions, solve their problems or give them the relief they seek?

Why Now?

Why is it important that they read this now?

Why Me?

Now you can talk about yourself. Why should they listen to you? What are your bonafides? Life experiences? Why should your readers trust you to help them resolve this issue together?

The 5 Parts of Your Book

Splitting Your Book

In this section, we will cover the five basic parts to every book. They are as follows:

1. Cover
2. Front Inserts
3. Chapters
4. Back Inserts
5. Back Cover

Within these 5 parts there are 19 sections. We will be diving into each section in full detail throughout these lessons so that you learn the exact *how to* for writing your book. They are as follows:

Part 1:

1. Cover – this is self-explanatory, but is very important as it is the first impression of your book.

Part 2:

2. What Others Are Saying About (Your

Name) and This Book – here is your chance to include positive reviews by those who have read your book.

3. Subtitle – this allows you to expand on the subject of your book or to use as a teaser.

4. Title Page – this is the inside page of your book which gives your title name.

5. Copyright Page – this gives the information as to your publisher and the protection afforded to the content of your book.

6. Dedication – this page highlights those people in your life who are important to you.

7. Acknowledgments – this page gives credit to those who have assisted you in your journey.

8. Contents – gives the reader the landscape of your book.

9. Preface (Optional) – gives the reader a taste of the how or why or what of your book.

10. Foreword (Optional) – a recommendation or positive review of your book that encourages a reader to spend the time and money to acquire and read your book.

11. Introduction – brings the reader into your subject or story by providing some

tidbit of information about it.

Part 3:

12. Chapters – this is the meat of your book.

Part 4:

13. Final Note or Thank you
14. Epilogue (Optional)
15. Appendixes (Optional)
16. About the Author
17. The Next Step

Part 5:

18. Back Cover

Title & Cover

Titles are important, but don't worry if you don't have one that you are 100% sure about when you start writing your book. There is plenty of time to make a final decision. So, just keep writing and believing that you will discover that great title exactly when you need it. In the meantime, let's go over some basic must haves.

Your cover should include:

1. Picture
2. Title
3. Subtitle
4. Your Name

Take a look at the books on your bookshelf. What intrigued you about those books? What about the cover caused you to take a second look? Think about these things as you decide on your title and cover. Ask the following questions:

Was it the message in the title?   YES   NO

The picture?   YES   NO

The subtitle?   YES   NO

Why did they interest you? Was it because of:

Emotion?   Yes   No

Mystery?   Yes   No

Was it a question?   Yes   No

Did it encourage you to do something?   Yes No

Was it funny?   Yes   No

As you think about your cover design, remember what moved you to pick up that book, turn it over and take to the counter to purchase it.

I'll give you an example from one of my own books:

Title: *100*

Subtitle: *100 Words in 100 Days to a Changed life and Restored Purpose.*

This book is a 100 day devotional and, at the time, I thought that the name "100" was a great name for my book. However, I learned from interacting with the public at different speaking events where my book was being sold, that people really didn't know what the book was about by the title. It didn't convey the type of book or give any clue to how to use it.

Now, once they looked through the book or spoke to me about the book they were engaged in the message, but before all of that, they really had no clue. That was a surprise to me, but it taught me a valuable lesson about the importance of titles and covers. So, if I decide to do a sequel to 100, I will go with something like this instead:

Title: *Get It All Back; Your Peace, Your Purpose & Your Prosperity.*

Subtitle: *A 100 Day Devotional*

So, while you have a moment, write down a couple of idea that you have for your book's title, knowing that you may change your mind a dozen times before you make your final decision.

Title:_____

Subtitle: _____

Title:_____

Subtitle: _____

Title:_____

Subtitle: _____

Now, let's move on to cover photos.

Self-Help Books

What is it that you are trying to help someone do, overcome or accomplish in their life by your book? Now, what does that look like in picture form? If you giving a message of overcoming depression, would you want to have a picture of someone who looks sad or looks happy? Or possibly a picture that shows someone in transition? Do you picture someone in a battle? What do you see? What would draw you in?

My advice in this area is to avoid something that is overdone. Think outside of the box and be creative.

Autobiography

This one is easy. Use a picture of yourself!

Fiction / Novel

What is the essence of your story? What feeling do you want to convey? Once you have the answers to these questions, think about what picture or image best exemplifies your message.

Children's Book

Make it something that would catch a child's attention. Consider the age range that you are going for and tailor it to fit what best excites and stimulates children in that particular grouping.

Documentary

Why should anyone be interested in this particular time or place that you are writing about? Show that through your picture choice. If it's about the ravages of war, show that. If it's about a beautiful unknown place that has a unique significance, put some aspect of the beauty of that place on the cover.

Start brainstorming right now...

This is what I would like my cover to convey:

_____
_____
_____
_____
_____
_____
_____
_____
_____
_____
_____
_____
_____
_____
_____
_____
_____
_____
_____
_____
_____
_____
_____
_____
_____
_____
_____

Practice designing your cover:

You can do it yourself or we can help.

Just as in any aspect of life you have options. You can design it yourself or you can elect to have it done by someone who specializes specifically in this field – Anointed Words Publishing Co. 800-496-4153 or awpubco.com.

Beginning Pages

Now let's talk about the pages that you may want to include before the actual meat of your book. We will take each on in the following order:

- Dedication
- Acknowledgments
- Contents
- Preface (Optional)
- Foreword (Optional)
- Introduction

Dedication Page

The *Dedication Page* is written to those who are integral to your life; those closest and dearest to you. This page, although probably the shortest of your beginning pages, should be your most personal, coming directly from your heart. Below are a few examples.

"I dedicate this book to my children who are my sunshine on stormy days."

"This book is dedicated to my husband/wife who never fails to make feel like I can accomplish anything."

Acknowledgments

This page in your book is where you acknowledge all those who have inspired you, assisted you or made a meaningful contribution to you achieving your goals in life. This is a place where you can give honor where honor is due.

Below, use the space to call to mind some of the people that you may want to include in your acknowledgement page.

People who have been in corner along the way:
1.
2.
3.
4.
5.
People who I have learned from or have inspired me on this journey:
1.
2.
3.

4.
5.

Contents

The contents page lists the order of the beginning pages, chapters, parts and ending pages in your book. This page is very important as it aids your potential reader in determining if they will make the decision to purchase your book and it helps those who already have your book find there place easily or skip to different sections in your book.

Preface

The Preface, should you choose to include one, is simply a message to your reader. It typically includes information about your book with a backstory or some specific piece of information that gives your reader some insight to the why or how of your book. For example; why will the reader benefit from this book? Why did I, the author, write this book and what qualifies me to write it? This can include educational or life experience, etc. Additionally, another way you can use the preface is to give the reader a little taste of the books story content or highlight a particular character.

Below is a list of all the topics I will include in my Preface:
1.
2.
3.
4.
5.

Foreword

This is a very good tool to use in your book and may often bring in readers that may have not yet made the decision to buy your book after reviewing the cover and the contents page. The foreword is not written by you, it is written by someone who will speak to the necessity or benefit of reading your book. Ideally, the person writing the foreword should have some standing or expertise in the topic or issue that you are writing about or they may be an established author that has a large following. The purpose of the foreword is to establish you and your book as one worthy of paying attention to. The foreword is essentially a book review or recommendation that will permanently be a part of your book, therefore choose this person or group of people carefully.

People I am considering to write my Foreword are:
1.
2.
3.
4.
5.

Here is a sample letter of request that you may want to send to the person that you would like to write your forward:

Dear _____,

I have just finished writing my new book, _____. This book seeks to _____ (*here, just list your goal or purpose for writing the book*). It would be a great honor if you would consider reading it, offering any critique or suggestions and writing a foreword which would be included in the book.

I have long admired your work in the area of _____ (*or state the reason why you are seeking their endorsement*). Thank you for your

consideration of this request and I will
completely understand if you decide to decline
at this time.

You can reach me by_____. Thank you
again and I hope to hear from you soon.

Yours truly,

Remember, this is just an example. You should
tailor your letter to match the relationship that you
have with the person that you are asking to write
your forward. If it is a friendly or personal
relationship, you may not want to be so formal in
your request and possibly ask them in person.

Introduction

Introduction

The Introduction is where you will first grab your reader's attention. In the introduction you will outline for the reader what you hope they will learn or achieve by reading your book. This section is about the reader, not about you the author.

There should be 8 paragraphs to your Introduction.

1. Attention Grabbing Statement
2. "I'm with you" Questions
3. I can relate Statement
4. Why Me?
5. Why I Care Statement
6. Action Statement

Examples of each paragraph if the book is a non-fiction book about recovering from abuse:

Attention Grabbing Statement: Statistics show that 8 out of 10 children that have been abused will become abusers themselves.

"I'm with you" Question: (this question is designed

to get your reader to say "yes" in agreement with you): If you have been abused or love someone who has, would you like to know how to not be a number in this statistic?

I Can Relate: (you relate or care): I know, all too well, how easy it is to fall into this trap.

Why me?: (what qualifies you): As a survivor of child sexual abuse, I have learned how not to be a statistic.

Why I Care: (why this is important to me and why I care about you): I took me years to learn that what happened to me wasn't my fault and I don't want you to lose years of happiness and purpose in your life when you don't have to.

Action Statement: (action plan): So, are you ready to get your life back and learn to love yourself again?

Practice writing each one. Just pick a topic and go…

1._____

_____

_____

2._____

_____

_____

3._____

_____

_____

4._____

_____

_____

5._____

_____

_____

6._____

_____

Chapters

Lessons

If you are writing a non-fiction book, the first step is to write down what you want your reader to learn from your book. For all others, you want to write down the key point or points that you want to give in that chapter as it relates to your overall story.

Take some time to write down the key lessons that you plan to give or the key parts of your story that each chapter will address. This will help you in your writing of the overall book and will also give you some idea as to the size of your book.

Here are a few spaces, but grab a piece of paper and add more.
1.
2.
3.
4.
5.
6.
7.
8.
9.

10.
11.
12.
13.
14.
15.
16.

After you have done that, group those lessons or points together with similar or like ones, but leave the ones that stand alone by themselves. From this grouping, you now have the basis of your chapters.

Below is an example from my book 'The Kingdom Wife':

1: Are wives struggling?
2: What are those struggles? (each struggle could be a chapter)
3: What are the sources of those struggles? (each source could be a chapter)
4: What can be done to overcome them?
5: Why we are victorious?

Every Chapter Should Have...

Every chapter should include:

A. Chapter Number

B. Chapter Title

C. The phrase, "In the last chapter we discussed...In this chapter we will cover..."

D. Inspirational quote

E. The lesson, specific subject or issue of this chapter

F. Summary Paragraph

A) Chapter Number

Your first chapter begins directly after your Introduction chapter.

B) Chapter Title

Make your chapter titles engaging and/or intriguing. Practice writing a few of your own:

1._____

2._____

3._____

C) The phrase, "In the last chapter we discussed…In this chapter we will cover…"

You don't have to use those exact words, but you definitely want to provide a bridge from the last chapter to the current chapter. Not only does it provide a smooth way of transitioning, but it will also aid the majority of readers who do not read an entire book in one sitting. This reminds them of what they just previously read and tells them where they are going. Everyone appreciates a roadmap.

D) Inspirational Quotes

You can quote someone else or make up your own. Just make sure that it is relevant to your chapter subject matter and not to lengthy as to defeat the purpose of providing a memorable thought or saying from your book. If you are quoting another person, be sure to give their name next to the quoted material.

Take some time to put your creative juices to work and think of a few powerful, catchy or memorable things you can say about the subject that you are considering writing about.

1._____

_____

2._____

_____

3._____

_____

E) The Lesson, Specific Subject or Issue of this Chapter

Here you want to introduce what this chapter is discussing specifically. Whether it is answering a question or introducing a specific issue or subject within your overall book, here is where you expand on that issue and tell the story and then provide the answer or action plan to bring resolution. If this is a fiction book, this would just be the next phase in your overall story.

Practice writing a couple of specific subject or issue sentences:

_____

_____

_____

_____

_____

F) Summary Paragraph

Now it's time to wrap up or summarize the major
points that you have discussed in the chapter. You
should be able to do this with just 2-3 sentences.

Try it:

_____

_____

_____

_____

_____

_____

Now what?

Start writing! The only way that your book will get finished and get to print is if you keep writing. I know that it can get discouraging, but now you have a blueprint that can help you stay focused and on track. Try to write at least 20 minutes a day, every day to start. You will be amazed at how much you can accomplish if you just stick to that minimal writing schedule. As you see your book come to fruition before your very eyes, you will quickly increase your writing time because you will become confident in your writing and become more engaged in the story that you are telling. I'm already excited for you!

Last, But Not Least

PART 4
BACK INSERTS
Final Note
Epilogue (Optional)
Special Reports (Optional)
Appendices (Optional)
About the Author
The Next Step

Final Note (optional/self-help books)
Use this page to encourage your readers to apply what they have learned.
Example:
Final Note
Responding to Fear Correctly
Your Final Note consists of 7 paragraphs. They are:
1. So Now What?
2. Challenge the Reader to apply what they learned.
3. Help them apply with a suggested action steps.
4. Summarize the book.
5. Offer to help them further?
6. Tell them how they can contact you .
7. Thank them for going on this journey with you and wish   them great success.

Practice writing something for each of the paragraphs (remember, all you need to make a paragraph is two sentences):

1._____

_____

_____

_____

2._____

_____

_____

_____

3._____

_____

_____

4._____

_____

_____

5._____

_____

_____

_____

6._____

_____

_____

_____

7._____

_____

_____

_____

Wonderful!

That's it...the secret to writing your amazing book fast!

I know that you will have great fun writing your book and that you will have a great sense of accomplishment when you have completed your project. It's your dream and you will achieve it.

So, once you're done, contact me at Anointed Words Publishing Company, and we'll help you get your amazing book to print.

God bless you as you write your anointed words!

A Few Other Book Links:

100: 100 Words in 100 days to a changed life & renewed purpose.
100 day devotional

The Kingdom Wife.
The Kingdom Wife (paperback)

I Declare! You're faith filled words have the power to change thing.
Everyday power declarations

OR VISIT:

leahmccray.com for this author
or
awpubco.com for publishing information

www.ingramcontent.com/pod-product-compliance
Lightning Source LLC
Chambersburg PA
CBHW071748020426
42331CB00008B/2225